The Story of Christ's Passion

A Tale for Children

by Anja-Sophia Henle

D1517768

For nearly four centuries, a Passion Play has been performed every ten years in the Bavarian village of Oberammergau. More than 2,000 of its residents take their places on the stage, of which 500 are children— and they naturally find the event very exciting. We have written this book for you so that you can read the story of Christ's Passion at home and learn about how the play is acted out.

Jesus travels to Jerusalem in the company of twelve of His best friends, His disciples, whom we know as the Twelve Apostles. In a village just outside the city, one of the disciples borrows a donkey, which Jesus rides on the last leg of the journey. Even though the donkey has never been ridden before, the animal remains calm and doesn't buck, not even once. Jesus doesn't ride the donkey because He is tired or lazy, but as a sign of His peaceful intentions. Everyone should see that Jesus does not want to harm anyone or anything. Many come out to meet Him when He arrives in the city. They have heard a great deal about Him and believe that He is to be their new king. This is why they are excited to see Him. They rejoice, shout with joy, and wave large, green palm leaves. Jesus pushes His way through the crowd, finally reaching the temple.

Jesus Arrives in Jerusalem

This is Frida. In the Passion Play, she is the donkey that Jesus rides into Jerusalem. Teaching her to act was no easy task. She would much rather graze on the nearby flowers than carry an actor around on stage. Yet she is usually very well behaved. The only thing Frida objects to is being petted on the head. When people try to do this, she gets very angry and sometimes even nips at her unsuspecting admirers.

More than 500 children from Oberammergau act in the Passion Play. They sing songs which they've rehearsed numerous times. When Christ enters Jerusalem, they stand near the front of the stage, cheering and waving their palm leaves. Even though they are terribly nervous before each performance—this is what actors call "stage fright"—the children always look forward to acting their roles.

Jesus Drives the Money-Changers Out of the Temple

When the actor playing Jesus tips over the tables and stalls in the temple, the commotion naturally frightens the doves away. Imagine how expensive it would be if new doves had to be bought for each performance! Luckily, they are tame and trained to fly back home to their dovecotes—just like carrier pigeons.

The little lambs also find it exciting to be on stage. But, when the noise and the commotion set in, they tremble with fear. Unlike people, the animals don't know that the scenes are being acted out—they think they are real. That's why they are happy when they can return safely to their field.

When Jesus arrives at the temple, He can't believe what He sees. A temple is to be a quiet place where people can pray in silence to God. But praying is no longer possible here. The entire temple is filled with stalls and booths, with money-changers and merchants standing behind them, selling animals that are to be sacrificed to God. The sheep baa, the goats bleat, and the doves coo. The money-changers shout loudly and the merchants haggle with their customers. The whole scene is chaotic, resembling a huge market. Jesus is angered by what He sees—by this misuse of the temple. He tips over the tables and stalls and drives away the traders.

He says to them: "It is written, 'My house shall be a house of prayer'; but you have made it a den of robbers" (Luke 19:46).

Jesus Preaches in the Temple

The Jewish high priest is called Caiaphas. He and the other priests are very angry, for they believe that Jesus has no right to drive the money-changers and merchants from the temple. But Jesus defends Himself. He also tells Caiaphas that compared to other people, no matter how many bad things they may have done, they are more likely to enter the Gates of Heaven than him. Jesus then turns and addresses the adults who are standing in front of the temple. He warns them to live as God would have it, and to set a good example for their children: "Truly, I say to you, unless you turn and become like children, you will never enter the Kingdom of Heaven. Whoever humbles himself like this child, he is the greatest in the Kingdom of Heaven" (Matthew 18:3-4). The crowd listens to Jesus very attentively. But the priests don't approve of this at all. They are envious of Him and, if given half a chance, they would throw Him into prison. But they don't dare do that, for the people would hate them for it. And the priests are afraid of being despised by the people.

This is the high priest, Caiaphas. He is played by the director's father, and it took him awhile to get used to walking around in a long robe and a huge hat. He was afraid that during the hot summer months when the play is performed he would break out into a sweat under such heavy garments. Can you believe that a man from Oberammergau traveled all the way to India to buy the fabric for these magnificent costumes?

As you can see, Jesus is very fond of children. He loves all people, regardless of whether they are rich or poor, always good or sometimes bad. People can sense Christ's love, and this is why they go to Him with their troubles, especially when they are ill. Jesus comforts and heals them. Astounded by His love, the people are powerfully drawn to Him.

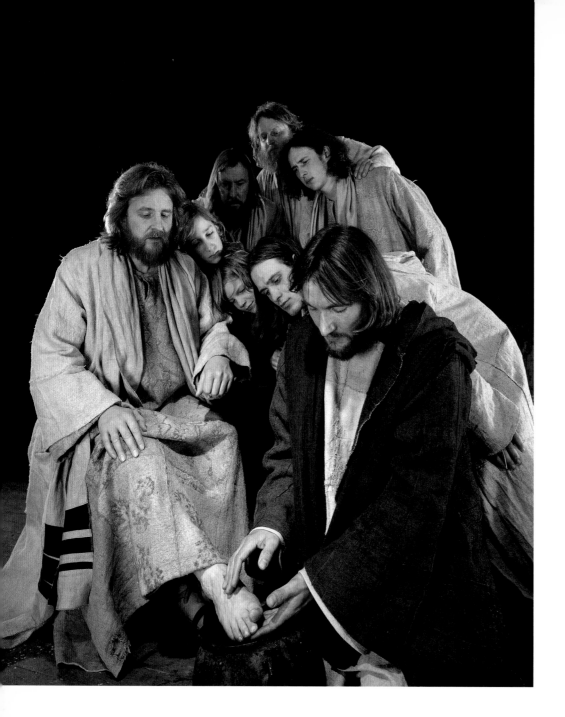

The Last Supper

Passover is the most important Jewish holy feast. Many hundreds of years before Christ was born, the Jews were held in exile and slavery in Egypt; they were freed through the special action of God and celebrated their liberation by feasting on roast lamb. This feast became part of the Jewish religious tradition, so that in Jesus' time, Jews invited their friends and family to their homes to eat roast lamb. Jews still do this today.

Jesus meets His disciples on the evening before the feast of the Passover. They are Jews and want to celebrate this Jewish feast together. But before they sit down at the table for their meal, Jesus, taking a towel and a large basin filled with water, begins to wash His disciples' feet. Peter is confused by this and asks Jesus to stop. But Jesus explains to Peter and the other disciples that He is teaching them that the master must be the servant of his fellows. This is a lesson that the disciples must learn. Then Jesus and the disciples sit down at the table. Jesus breaks a loaf of bread, distributes it among the Disciples, and says: "This is my body which is given for you" (Luke 22:19).

Afterwards He takes a cup of wine and passes it around the table, and then He says: "Drink of it, all of you; for this is my blood of the covenant, which is poured out for many for the forgiveness of sins" (Matthew 26:27–28).

His friends listen and are confused. What does He mean? Jesus explains to them that He will soon die—that one of them will betray Him to His enemies, who will put Him put to death. Jesus' disciples all proclaim that they will never betray Him. Judas, one of the disciples, asks Him whether he is the betrayer. "Yes," answers Jesus. Judas then leaves.

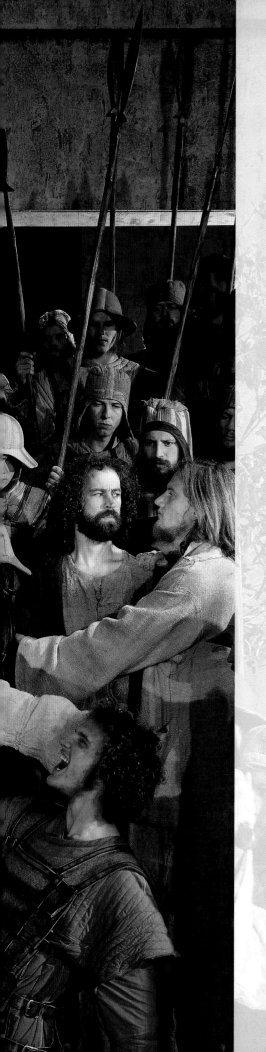

Judas betrays his friend Jesus to His enemies, just as Christ had said.
Why does Judas do this? Is it just for the money? Perhaps he would like
to force Jesus to prove His strength. He wants Jesus to demonstrate just
how strong He really is—powerful enough to resist the soldiers.

Jesus Is Taken Prisoner

After the Last Supper, Jesus walks to the Mount of Olives with His friends. The mountain was given this name because of the many olive trees that grew there. It is already dark and the disciples are afraid of what is to come. Jesus knows how terrible the suffering will be. In anguish, He begs God that He might be spared, nevertheless He prays: "Not my will, but thine, be done" (Luke 22:42). Jesus comforts His disciples and offers them strength. But He also warns them that they, too, will be persecuted, for being His friends. The disciples give Him their word that they will stand by Him, no matter what happens. But Jesus knows better. He says to Peter: "Before the cock crows, you will deny me three times" (Matthew 26:75). Suddenly they hear something. A group of soldiers is approaching. Their torches can be seen in the distance. Who is leading them? None other than Judas! He greets Jesus with an embrace and kisses Him on the cheek. This was the sign agreed upon by Judas and the enemy, so that they would know which of the men was Jesus. The soldiers arrest Him and lead Him away. In an effort to protect Jesus, Peter draws his sword and cuts off Malchus's right ear, who is one of the high priest's servants. What a terrible thing to do! Although Peter only wants to help his friend, Jesus does not approve. Instead, He lays His hand on Malchus and heals him, for Jesus does not want people to treat each other cruelly and brutally. Not even their worst enemies.

Jesus Is Brought Before Annas

The soldiers bring the prisoner Jesus before Annas. Even though Peter is frightened, he follows them and waits in front of the gates of the palace where Jesus is being tried. Shortly thereafter, Jesus is led back outside. Annas's servant strikes Jesus, whose eyes are blindfolded with a cloth. One of the soldiers strikes Him again, and he calls out: "Prophesy! Who is it that struck you" (Luke 22:64). For they believe that, if Jesus were really a prophet, as many claim, He should be able to recognize the person, blindfolded or not. But they fail to understand what a prophet is. He is not simply someone with supernatural powers. He is a visionary. He can see more clearly than other people what is happening in the world and why many things go awry. This has nothing to do with fortune-telling or magic. During the entire time of Jesus' persecution, Peter is nearby but he does not dare utter a word. When he is asked if he is a friend of the prisoner, Peter replies: "I do not know not this man of whom you speak" (Mark 14:71). The people ask him on two more occasions if he is a follower of Jesus. Again, he denies it. After the third time, the cock crows. Do you remember that, on the previous evening, Jesus foretold precisely this turn of events? Peter remembers too, and begins to weep bitterly.

Peter is sad because he has betrayed his best friend. He did not think himself capable of doing such a horrible thing. But he was so afraid that he, too, would be taken prisoner. That was the only reason why he claimed not to know Jesus. Most people would probably have acted as Peter did in that situation—even though they, too, might feel terribly ashamed of themselves afterwards.

Jesus Before Caiaphas and the High Council

Jesus is led away to Caiaphas, the high priest, who asks Him many questions. He asks Jesus if He is the Messiah, to which He makes no reply. Jesus remains silent and does not defend Himself. Then they ask Him: "Are you the Son of God, then?" and He answers: "You say that I am" (Luke 22:70). The word "messiah" means "the anointed one," and, in those days, only kings were anointed. This statement by Jesus is what confirms the Council in their opinion that Jesus is an agitator and a blasphemer. For this reason, they believe He should be condemned to death. Only one of the priests defends Jesus; all the others demand that He be put to death. They are relieved finally to have found an excuse for such a harsh judgment, for there are several reasons why they fear Jesus will make Himself the King of the Jews. For one thing it would mean that the priests would not have as much power as before. For another they are afraid that it would mean the end of peace in Israel, for, in those days, Israel was not an independent country, but was ruled by the Romans, who never would have accepted Jesus as the King of the Jews. They would have fought Him and His followers. When Judas learns that Jesus is to be crucified, he is beside himself. He regrets having betrayed his friend and feels responsible for Jesus' fate. Judas is so miserable that he no longer wants to live. He takes a rope and hangs himself.

Do you see how magnificent the robes of the high priests and the High Council are?
In contrast, the simple folk wear plain beige or brown garments. The Passion Play's costume
designer planned this intentionally so as to show just how powerful and rich Caiaphas and
his peers were.

Some parts of the story
reenacted in Oberammergau
are very sad and terrifying. If
you go to the play and are
frightened, then just close
your eyes. Remember: it's
only a play! Nothing will
really happen to the actor
who plays Judas. When the
play is over, he will go home
just as happy and healthy as
everyone else.

Take a closer look at the costumes which Herod and his followers are wearing. They consist of thousands of chicken feathers that have been dyed black. The costume designers needed a long time to affix each and every feather. Isn't the effect spectacular?

Jesus Is Brought Before Pontius Pilate and Herod

The high priest Caiaphas doesn't have the authority to sentence Jesus to death. First, Pontius Pilate must give his consent, for Pilate is the Roman governor of Jerusalem and thus the most powerful man in the city. The priests lead the prisoner to Pilate, who did not get on at all with Caiaphas. Pilate then questions Jesus and, not finding that He has done anything wrong, decides that Jesus should be released. But the priests put pressure on Pilate, who then commands that Herod be the judge of Jesus, for Herod is King of Galilee, the province in which Jesus was born. But Herod is a bad king who spends his time amusing himself and avoiding his work. Herod makes fun of Jesus and tells Him to perform some miracles. When Jesus neither floats in the air nor turns a staff into a snake, Herod places a scarlet robe on Him and calls Him cruel names. Then he sends all who are present back to Pilate. The story is getting more and more complicated. Up to now, no one has been prepared to condemn Jesus to death. But the priests remain persistent.

Jesus Is Flogged

Jesus is once again brought before Pontius Pilate, who is slowly but surely losing his patience. He is still not willing to have Jesus crucified. He is afraid that the people might be angry and rise up against him. Neither is he eager to do what the priests desire of him. He wants to show that he is the most powerful man in Jerusalem, the one who makes the decisions. That is why he orders that Jesus should be taken away and flogged—or scourged—which the soldiers do willingly. They relish their power over Jesus, for normally they are unimportant people who must obey the orders of their superiors. They smite and beat Him brutally, until His blood-stained body collapses. Still, they continue to torture Jesus. They place a crown of thorns upon His head and mock Him, calling out: "Hail! King of the Jews!" (Matthew 27:29).

It is hard to believe how cruel people can be—and that does not just go for people of earlier times. Today, many innocent people are still tortured in wars, as well. The actor playing Jesus, of course, is not really beaten. The blood covering his body is only paint. And, even though the sound of the soldiers' whips is terrifying, the blows don't actually hit the actor's body, but the ground instead.

Pontius Pilate Condemns Jesus to Death

Caiaphas presses Pilate to pronounce the death sentence. Because there is a yearly custom in honor of the Passover that one prisoner be pardoned at the request of the people, Pilate suggests that he release Jesus. The other alternative would be to release Barabbas. Pilate wants to avoid this at all costs, for he considers this criminal to be far more dangerous than Jesus. But, the priests demand: "Away with this man, and release unto us Barabbas" (Luke 23:18). Pilate is in a dilemma. He is too much of a coward to impose his will on the priests. So he declares that the people should decide. Naturally, Caiaphas tries to convince as many people as possible to condemn Jesus. And, although Jesus' friends try to win supporters for their cause, the majority shout for the release of Barabbas instead. Although Pilate doesn't want to—and he knows that Jesus has committed no crime—he condemns Him to death. Pilate has a basin of water brought to him and washes his hands, saying: "I am innocent of this man's blood; see to it yourselves" (Matthew 27:24). Caiaphas and his followers have finally achieved what they wanted: Jesus is to be crucified.

You have no doubt heard the expression "to wash your hands of something." What this means is: "Alright, I will do as you wish. But don't blame me for it later." Pilate knows that Jesus is innocent. He nevertheless has Jesus put to death. This is cowardly and unjust, and Pilate does not want to take responsibility for the death of Jesus. To indicate this, he washes his hands before the multitude.

Jesus Carries the Cross

Although Jesus has already undergone the cruelest of torture, He must now carry His own cross up a steep hill outside the city. The hill is called Calvary, or Golgotha, which means "skull," for the hill is shaped like a skull. Jesus is exhausted and finds the cross extremely heavy to bear. Yet He doesn't complain. Not once. The saddest part is that very few of His friends accompany Him. John is the only disciple who stays with Him. Mary, His mother, and the other women will also not be deterred from accompanying Him in this dark hour. When Jesus collapses, one of the soldiers orders Simon, who is nearby, to carry the cross. A woman named Veronica, whose heart is filled with sorrow when she sees Jesus, wipes the blood and sweat from His face with a cloth.

Can you see how huge the cross is that Jesus must carry up the hill? It must have been a terrible burden for Him. The cross in Oberammergau Passion Play is also extremely large and heavy. The actors who play the role of Jesus must be very strong indeed!

Jesus Is Crucified

Having reached the top of the hill the soldiers nail Jesus and two thieves to the crosses. Above the head of Jesus, Pilate has a sign affixed to the cross that reads "INRI," meaning "Jesus of Nazareth, The King of the Jews." In agony, Jesus exclaims: "Father, forgive them; for they know not what they do" (Luke 23:34). The soldiers cast lots for the clothes of the crucified Christ. But He doesn't despise His worst enemies. No, Jesus even prays for them. After much suffering, He cries out, "Father, into thy hands I commend my spirit" (Luke 23:46), and dies. Suddenly the sky becomes very dark and it begins to thunder. Everyone is frightened, including the Roman soldiers, who are not easily scared. They say to each other: "Certainly this man was innocent!" (Luke 23:47). To be quite sure that Jesus is dead, the soldier Longinus takes a lance and pierces His side. Jesus' body is taken down from the cross and Caiaphas dictates that He should be buried in a grave designated for criminals. But Joseph of Arimathea, a follower of Jesus, obtains permission to bury him in a tomb hewn out of rock. To close off the tomb, a large, heavy stone is placed at the entrance.

It is not easy to reenact the nailing of Christ to the cross. The scene must appear real, but, of course, the actor can't be hurt, and so mountain climbing equipment is hidden under his loin cloth. This includes a ring that is hooked onto the cross and sustains most of his weight. This way he is certain not to fall off! And his feet rest on a small ledge. When the soldiers "nail" Jesus to the cross they actually hammer the nails only into the wood and not Jesus' hands! At the same time, they spray fake blood on his body, making the whole event look very real. The actors are so skilled that the audience doesn't notice what is really happening— even if they watch closely.

Jesus Is Risen!

The tomb of Jesus is guarded by three soldiers. They have been sent by the priests who fear that His body might be stolen as proof that He has risen from the dead. Three days after the Crucifixion the women return to anoint the body of Jesus. The guards, however, do not want to let them near the body. Mary Magdelene looks past one of the guards and, seeing that the great stone that sealed the tomb has been rolled away, exclaims: "They have taken the Lord out of the tomb" (John 20:2). The guards don't know what to do. They are certain that no one could have reached the tomb without passing them. Yet, they also see that the body has disappeared and that the cloth in which it was wrapped lies neatly folded together. At this moment, a shining angel appears to the distressed women and reassures them: "Do not be afraid; for I know that you seek Jesus who was crucified. He is not here; for He has risen, as He said. Come, see the place where He lay. Then go quickly and tell His disciples that He has risen from the dead" (Matthew 28:5–7). The women are overjoyed and immediately leave to spread the good news of the miracle.

The Passion story is a very sad tale. You'll have noticed that. But it has a happy ending: Jesus lives! Christ rose from the dead. The play in Oberammergau finishes here, with Jesus appearing one more time on stage. The spectators are overwhelmed by the powerful turn of events. You can read more about how the story continues in the Bible. It tells how Jesus appears to His friends many more times. He shows them that He has not deserted them and that He will always be with them. That's a wonderful feeling, isn't it? That is why Christians far and wide celebrate Easter as the most important time of the year and as the beginning of their religious calendar.

This is Anton and Martin. They take turns playing the part of Jesus, every other day. It's important that two actors can play the role. Imagine how difficult it would be if there were only one actor each for Jesus, Mary or Caiaphas. They would have to act the part nearly six hours every day! And what would happen if they were sick and had to stay in bed? Then the performance would have to be canceled. That would leave the many people who travel to Oberammergau just to see the play very disappointed.

play every ten years if they were spared. It is said that from this time on, not a single person died of the plague! The residents were so thankful that they kept their promise the very next year. In the local graveyard they erected a temporary stage of wooden planks and began to act out the story. Later they built a large theater that held 4,000 people. Nowadays, the Passion Play is famous around the world, and thousands of visitors come to the small Bavarian village every ten years to see it performed.

The History of the Oberammergau Passion Play

The Passion Play has been performed in Oberammergau for a long time. About 400 years ago, that is, in 1633, the "Black Death" plague spread quickly across southern Germany. The inhabitants of Oberammergau were afraid of the contagious disease, which caused the death of thousands of people. That is why the residents of the village vowed to God that they would perform the Passion